How to Draw Guns Step-by-Step Guide

Best Gun Drawing Book for You and Your Kids

BY

ANDY HOPPER

Copyright Notes

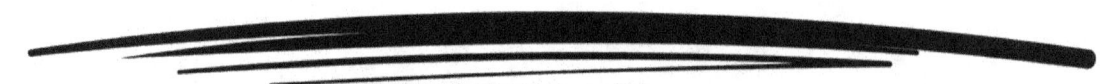

Table of Contents

Introduction...4

How to Draw a DP12 Shotgun..5

How to Draw a FN Five Seven Pistol...........................24

How to Draw a FN P90 Rifle..40

About the Author 57

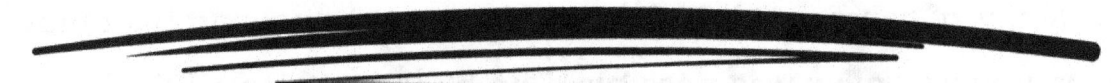

Introduction

Kids have this intense desire to express themselves the ways they know how to. During their formative years, drawing all sorts is on top of their favorite things to do. You ought to encourage as it boosts their creativity and generally advances their cognitive development.

This book is written to give you and your kids the smoothest drawing experience with the different guides and instructions on how to draw different kinds of objects and animals. However, you should note that drawing, like everything worthwhile, requires a great deal of patience and consistency. Be patient with your kids as they wade through the tips and techniques in this book and put them into practice. Now, they will not get everything on the first try, but do not let this deter them. Be by their side at every step of the way and gently encourage them. In no time, they will be perfect little creators, and you, their trainer.

Besides, this is a rewarding activity to do as it presents you the opportunity of hanging out with your kids and connecting with them in ways you never knew was possible. The book contains all the help you need, now sit down with them and help them do this.

That is pretty much all about it - we should start this exciting journey now, shouldn't we?

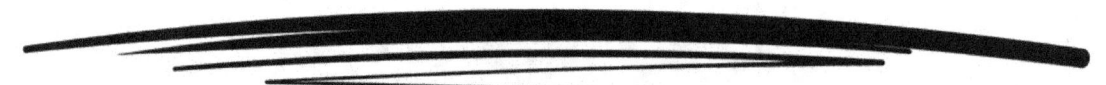

How to Draw a DP12 Shotgun

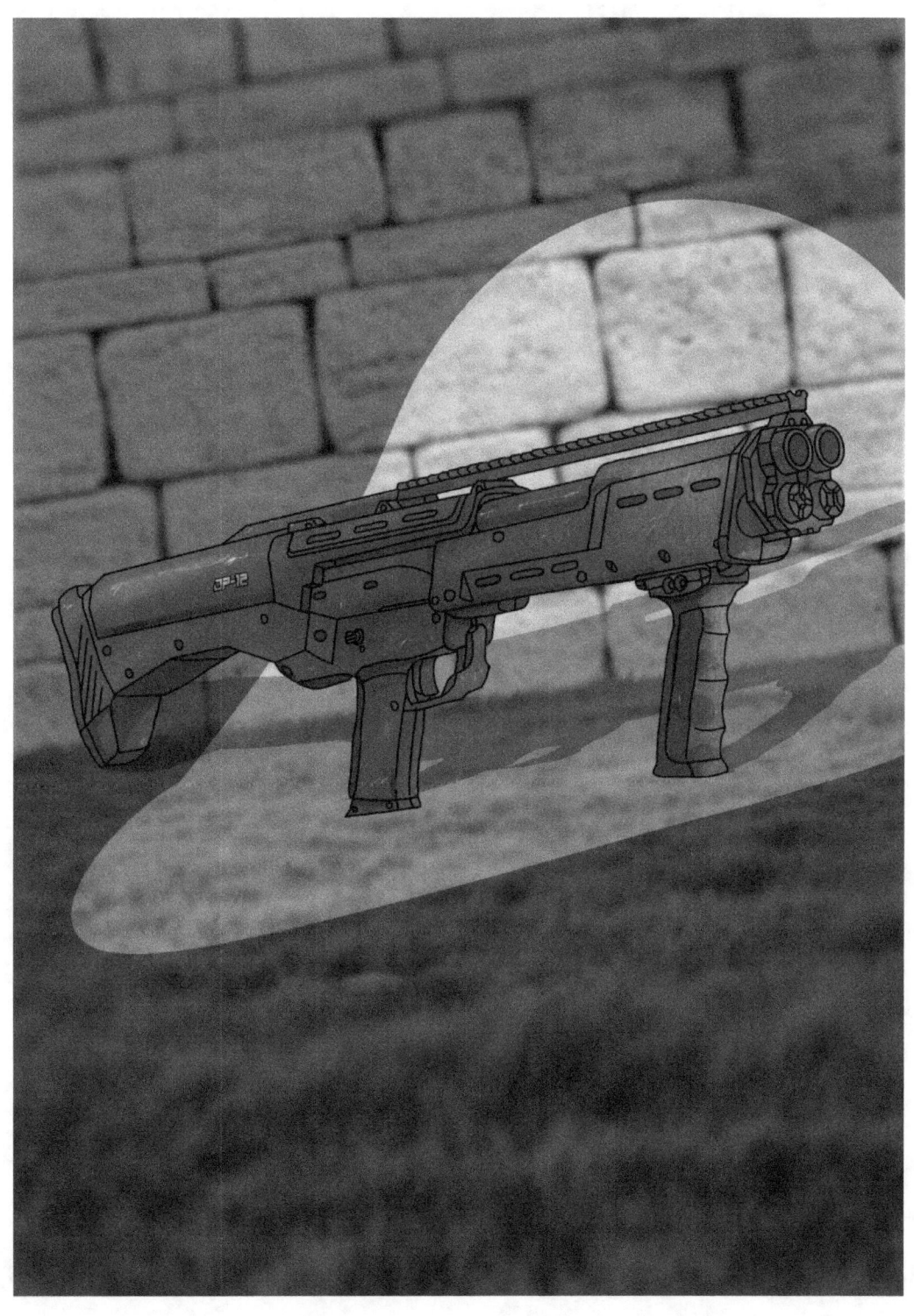

Step 1.

To start we will make the outline for the barrel, the handles, the visor and the shoulder support.

Step 2.

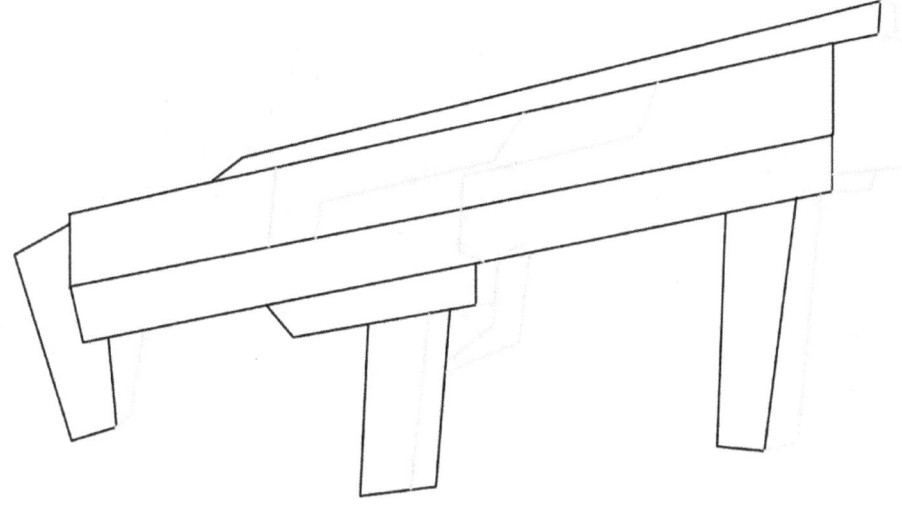

Add the front part of the shotgun to give the outlines a 3 dimensional appearance. Add lines inside to separate parts of the outline.

Step 3.

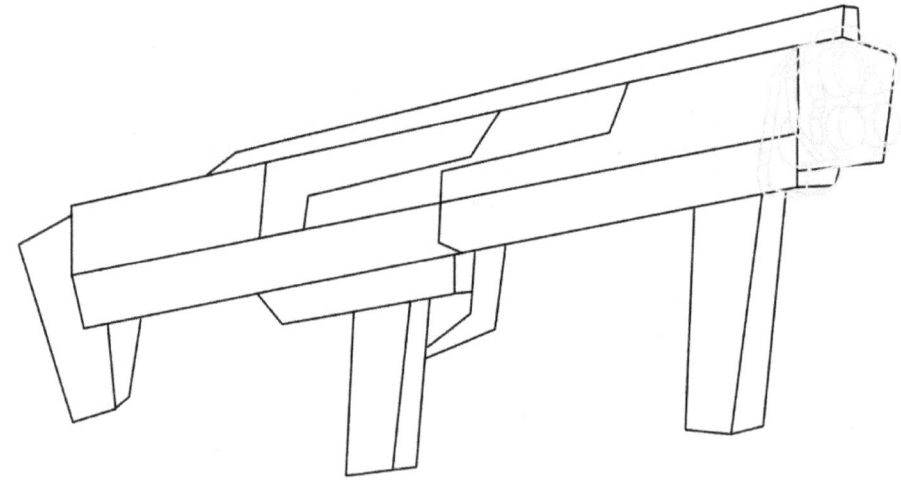

Move to the front of the shotgun and add the barrels on the
outside at the top, with the support right below it. Add the
support around the barrel to attach it to the shotgun.

Step 4.

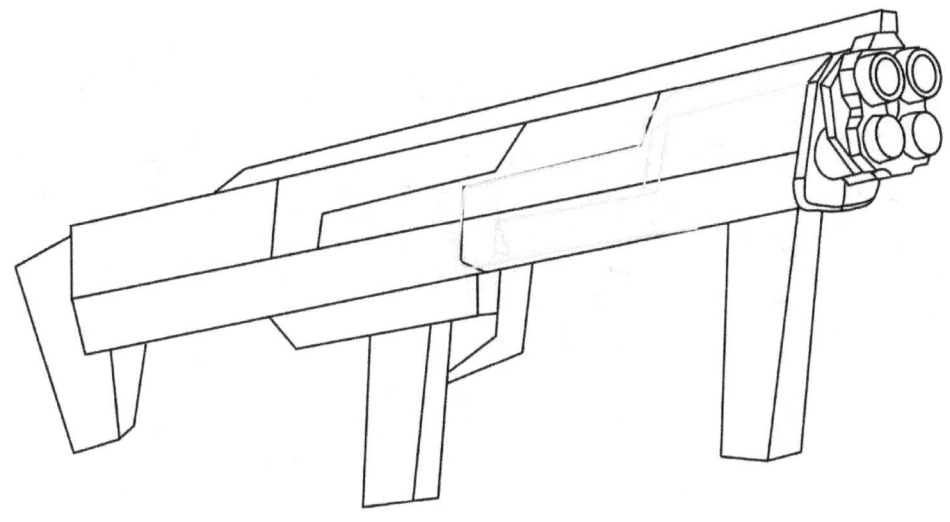

Add the outline of the front part of the gun as in the example.

Step 5.

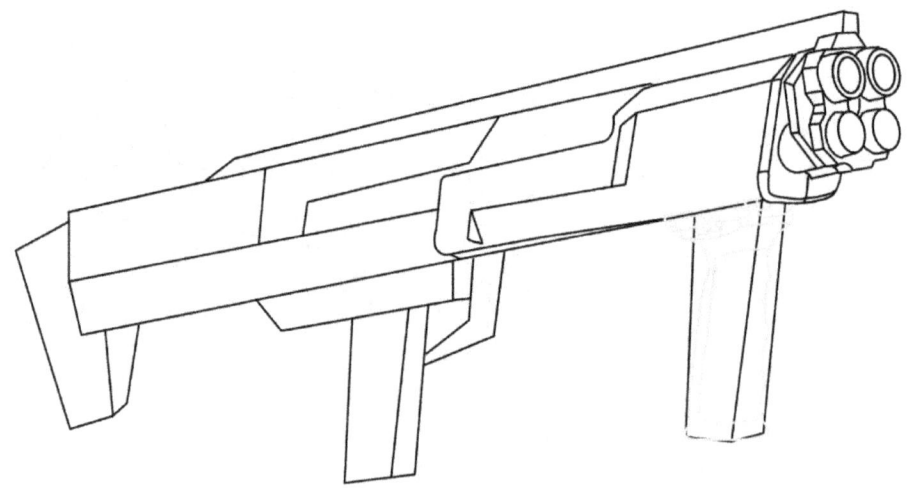

Now redraw the front handle. Add the bolts at the top to secure
it to the body of the shotgun.

Make sure to wave out the side of the handle to show where the
fingers should wrap around the handle.

Step 6.

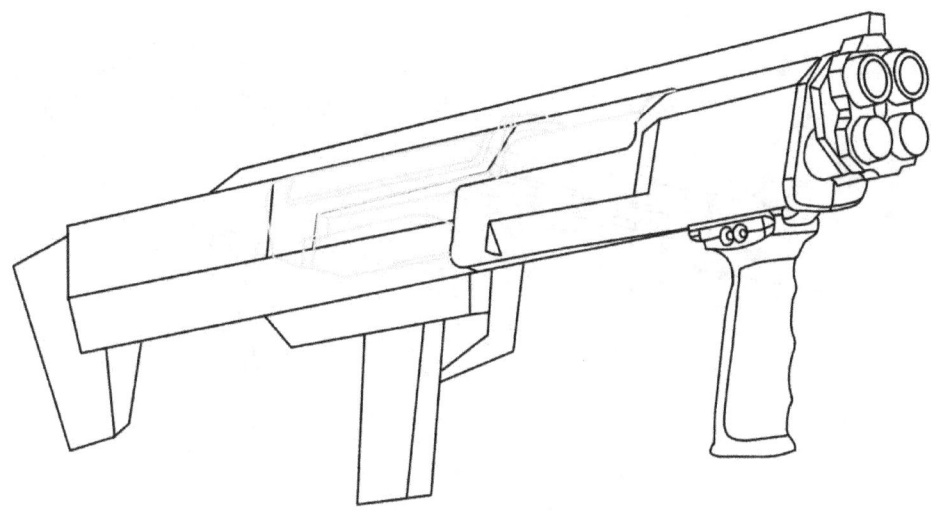

Now redraw the section where the barrel where the bullets sit.

Make sure to use the example to show where to curve the

support.

Step 7.

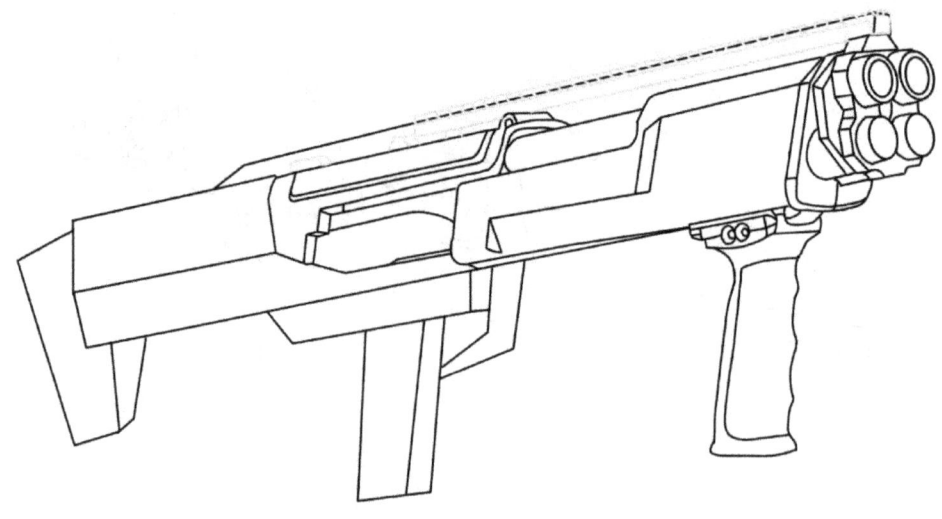

Now redraw the visor up top. See how the side looks like the
top of a wall of a castle?

Step 8.

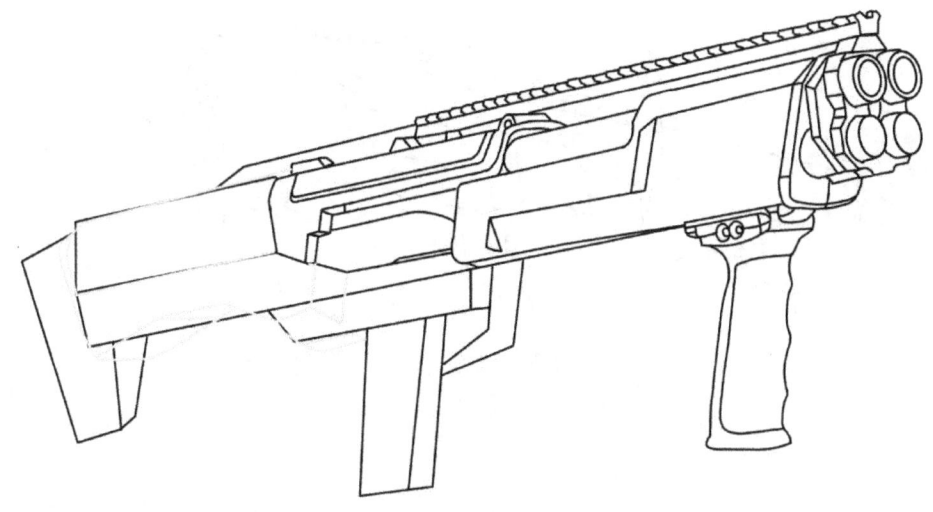

Now redraw the back of the body to give it a slicker shape. See
how it's slowly coming together?

Step 9.

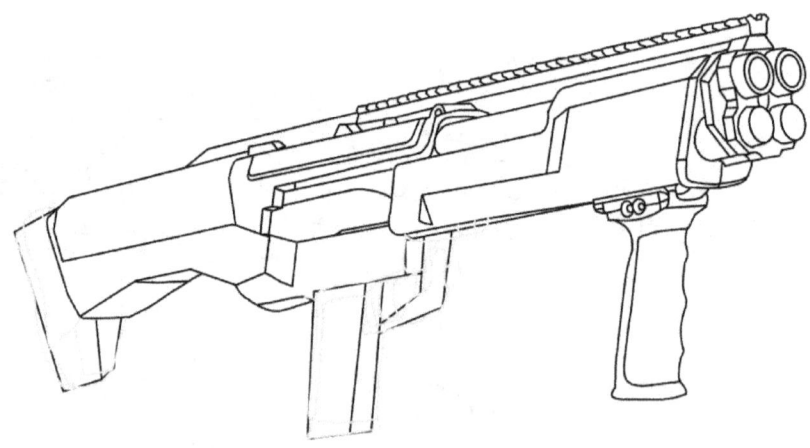

Now redraw the shape of the shoulder support, rounding it out
to make it fit the shape of the human body.

Then redraw the trigger mechanism and the cover surrounding
it.

Now continue with redrawing the handle underneath it,
rounding it out to fit the hand.

Step 10.

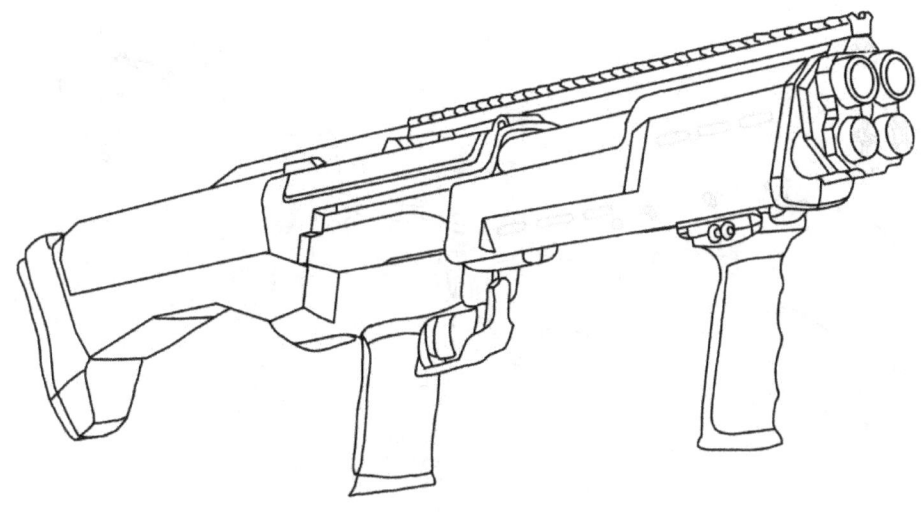

Add the details to the front of the body. Such as the ventilation shafts and the decal on the very front.

Step 11.

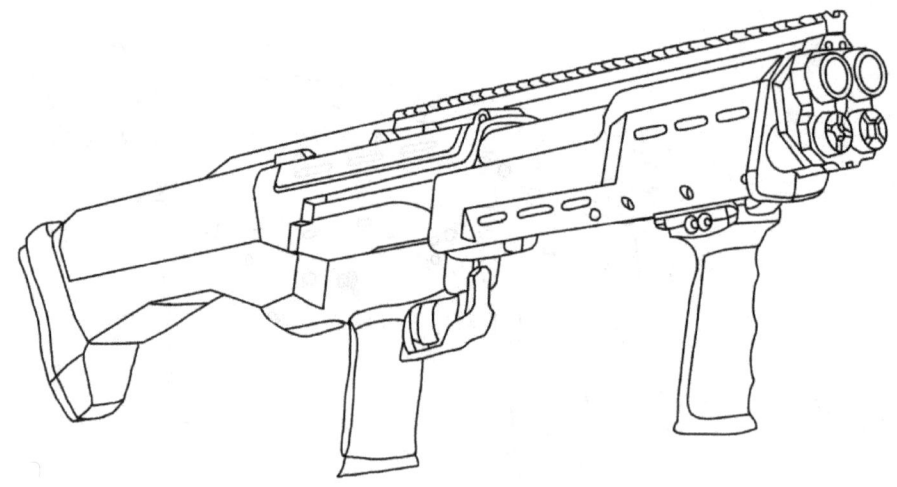

Now do the same for the midsection of the body. Add the safety valve down the middle, With circles for the bolts that hold the body together.

Step 12.

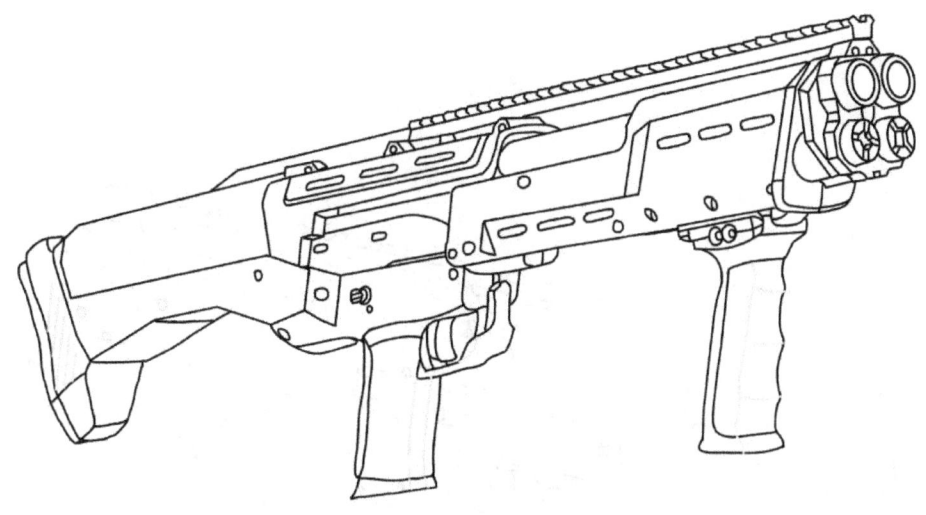

Now finish the shoulder support and the handles as in the example.

Step 13.

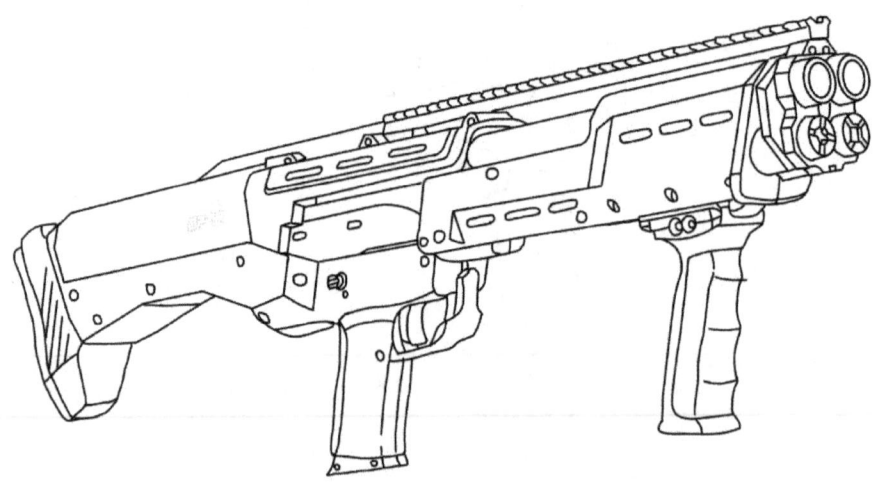

Lastly, Add the DP-12 logo on the back of the shotgun.

Step 14.

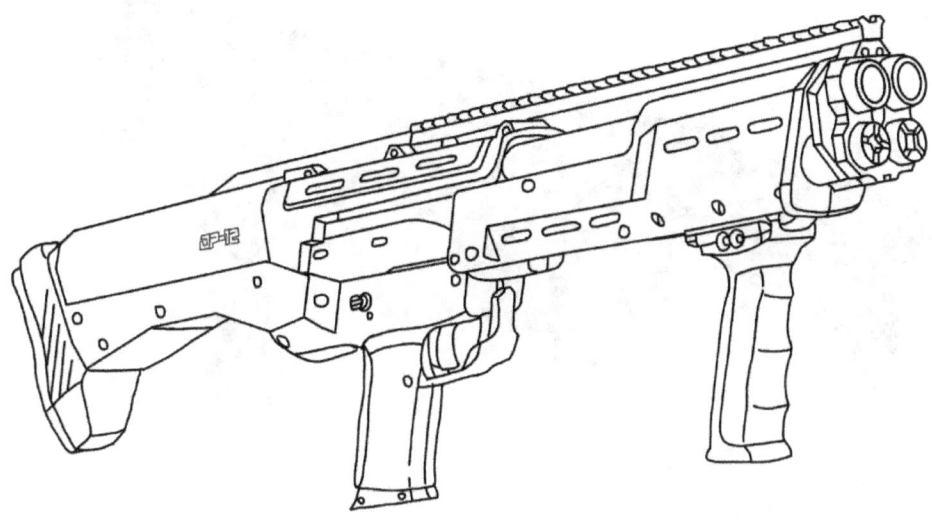

All done! Let's color!

Step 15.

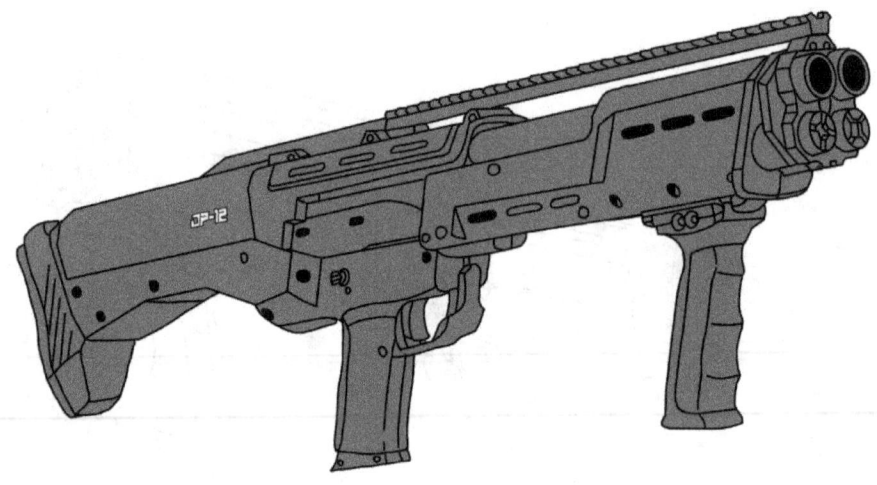

The shotgun is a mono-color. Color it dark grey.

The logo is all white.

Step 16.

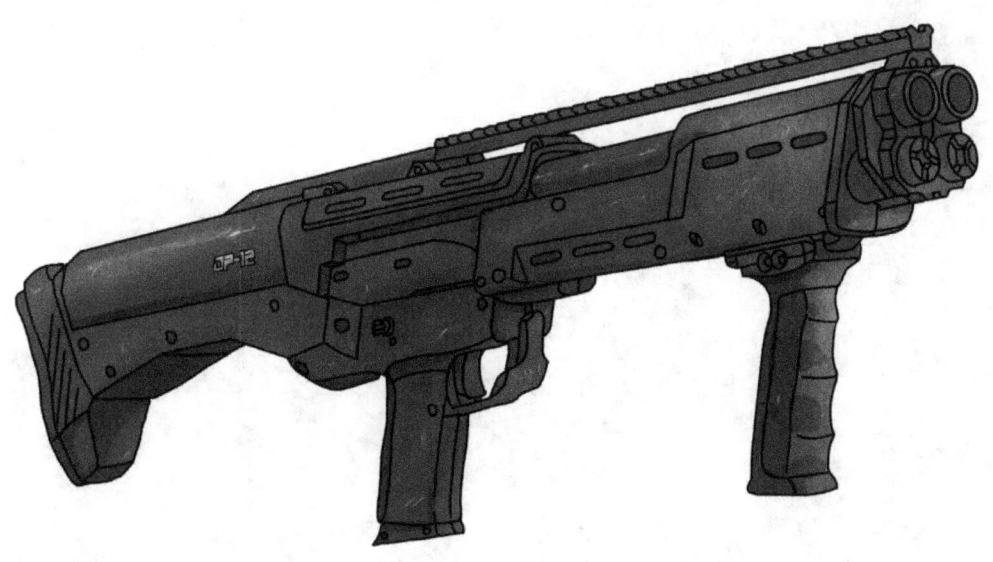

Add some color and scratches for detail. How does yours look?

Step 17.

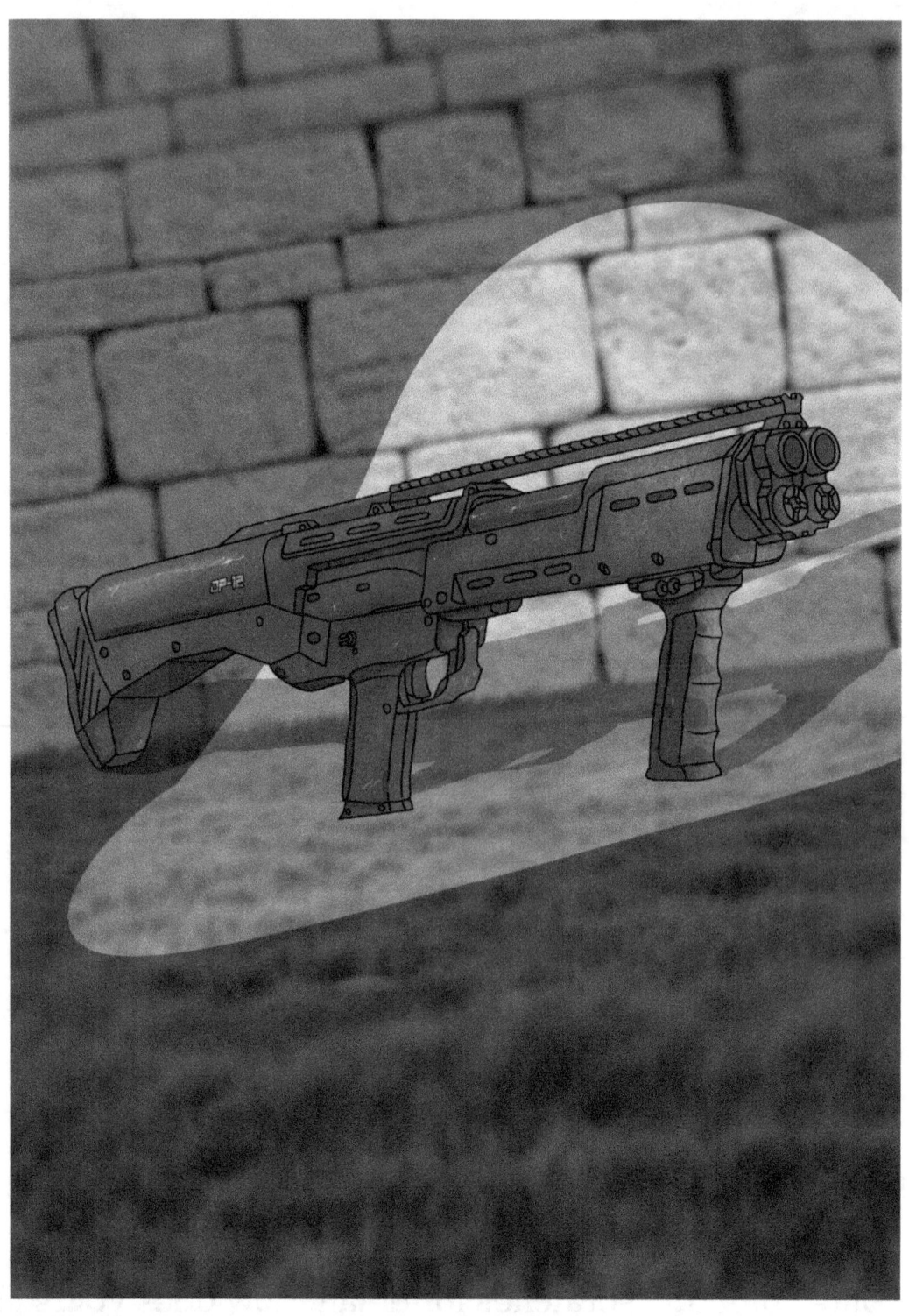

Colored version.

Step 18.

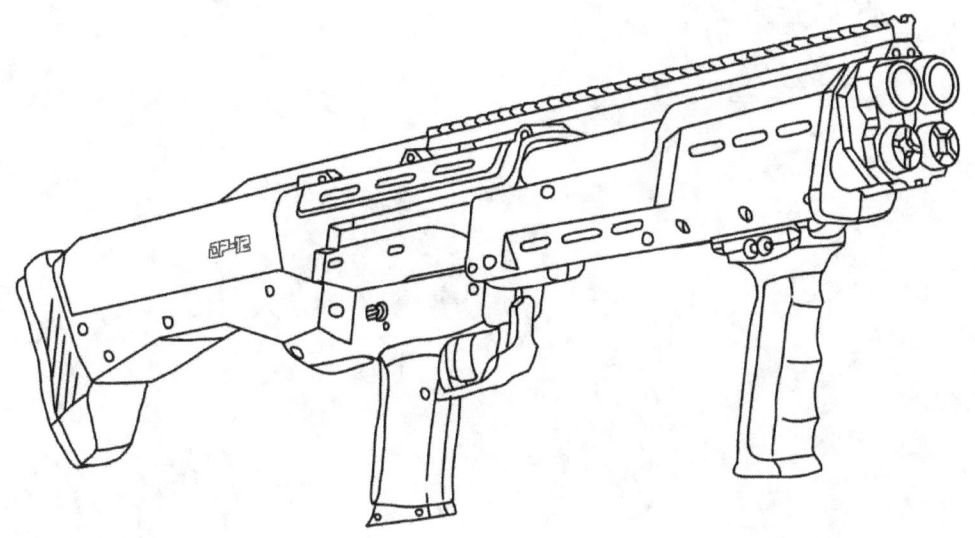

Line art version.

How to Draw a FN Five Seven Pistol

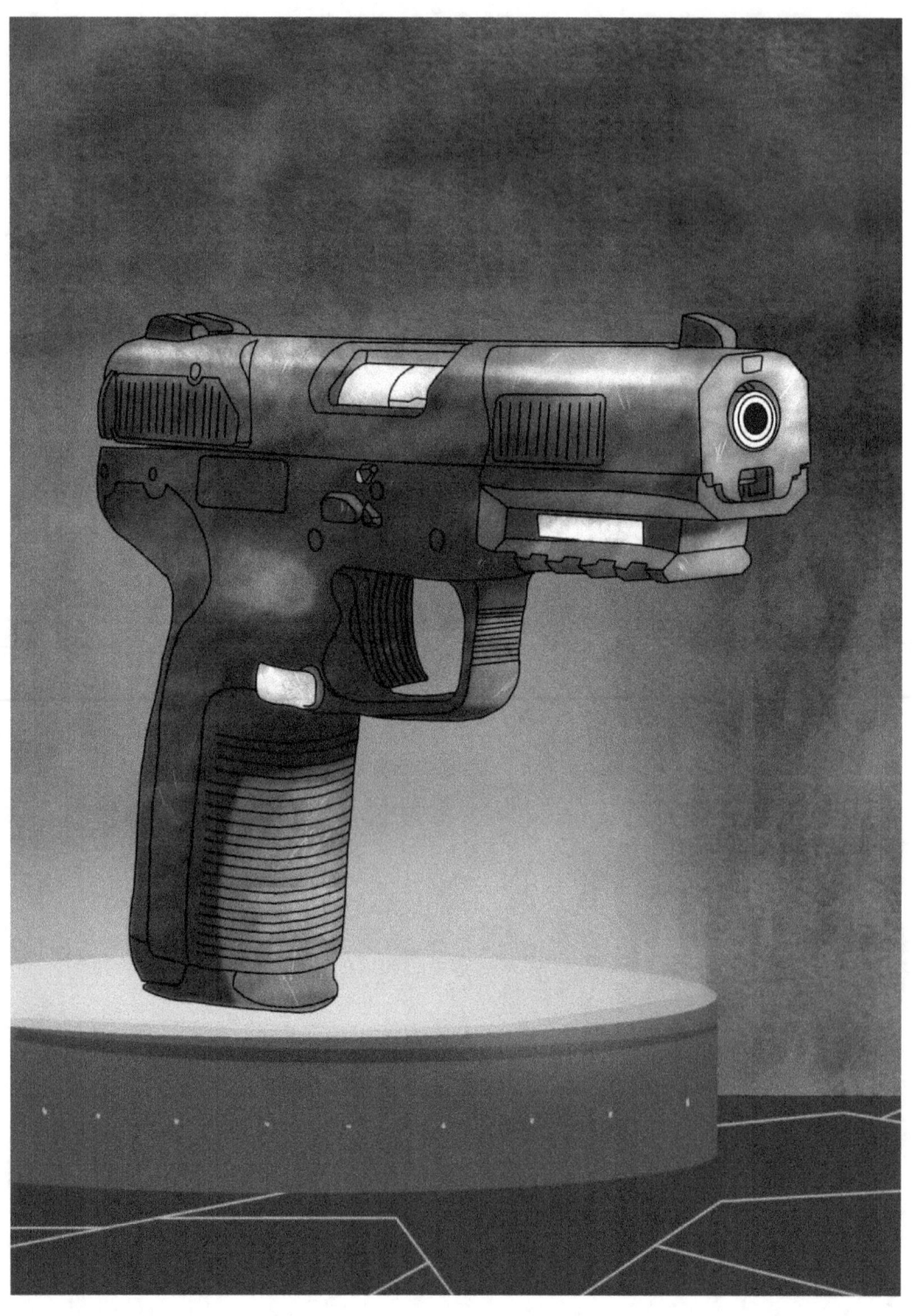

Step 1.

To start we will make the outline for the barrels and the handle.

Step 2.

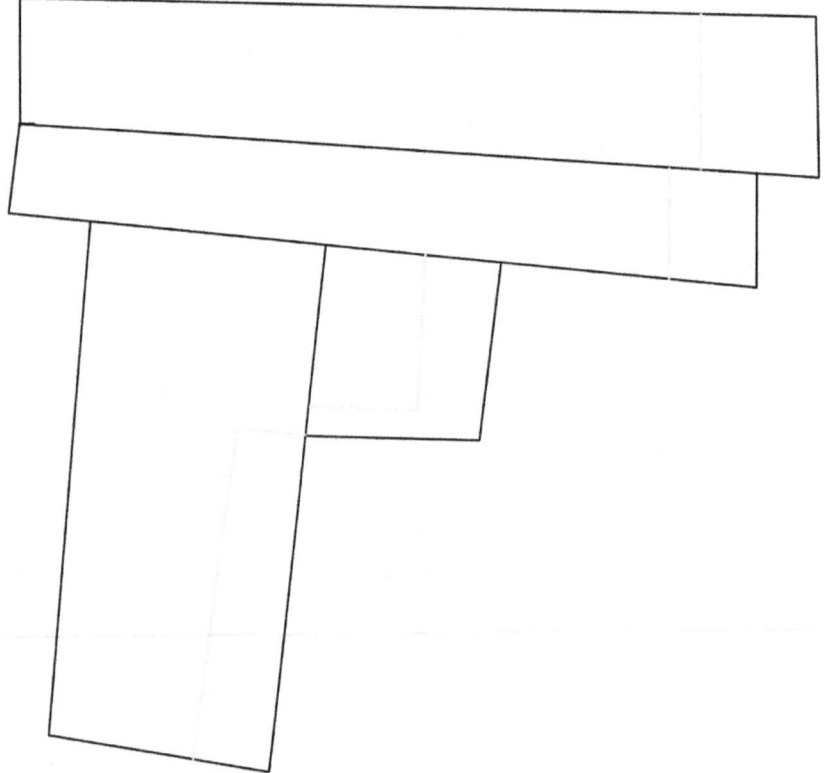

Add the front part of the pistol to give the outlines a 3 dimensional appearance. Add lines inside to separate parts of the outline.

Step 3.

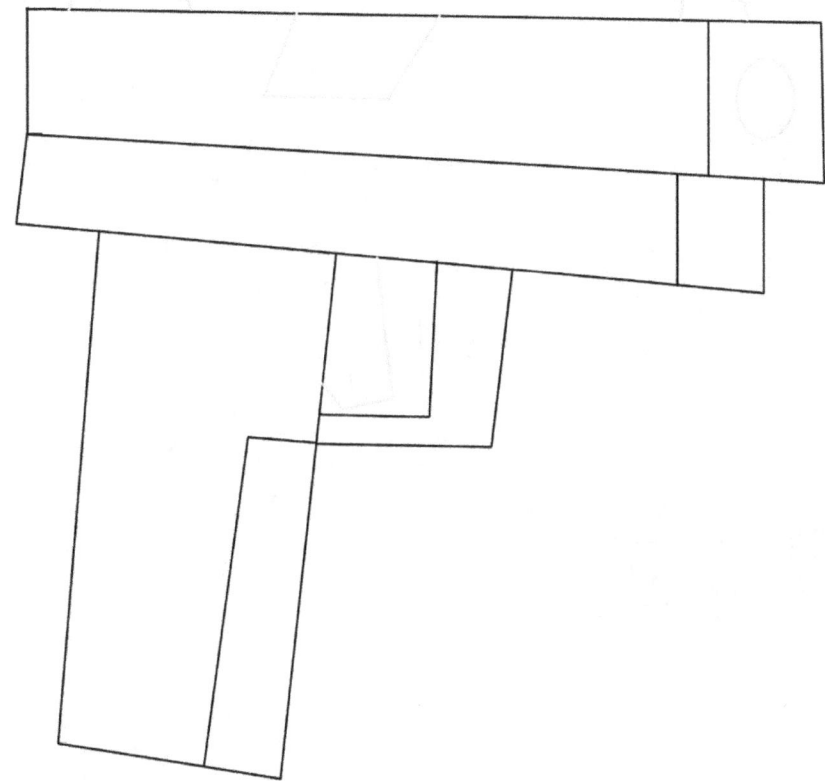

Add the outline of the visor on top, the trigger in the center, the shaft where the bullet flies out of, and the barrel at the front.

Step 4.

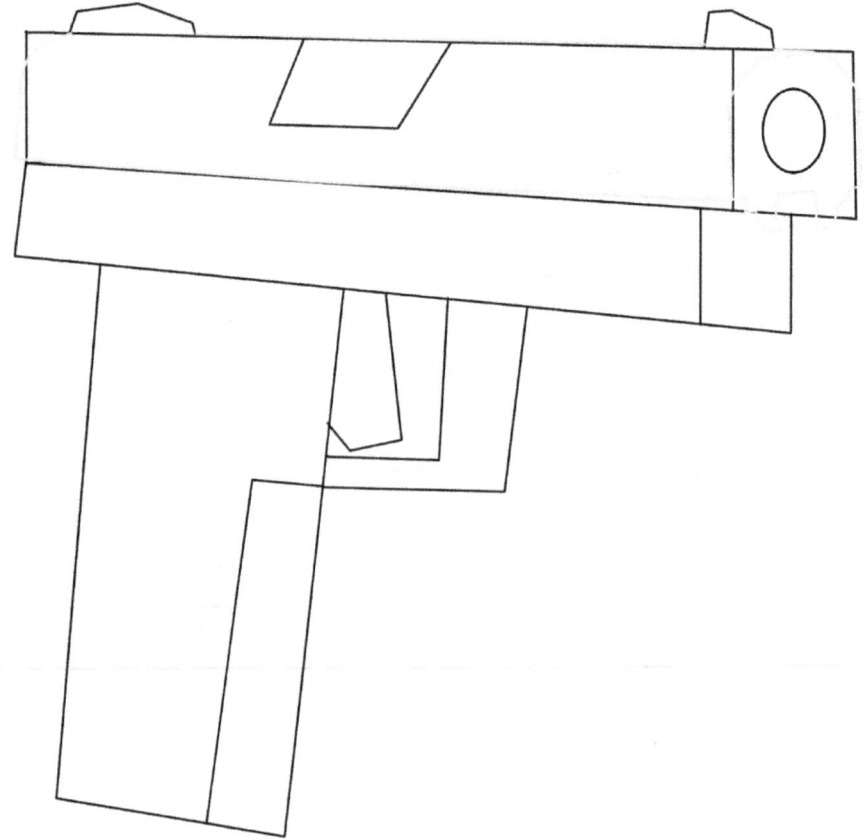

Redraw the top part of the gun to give it a 3dimensional shape.

Step 5.

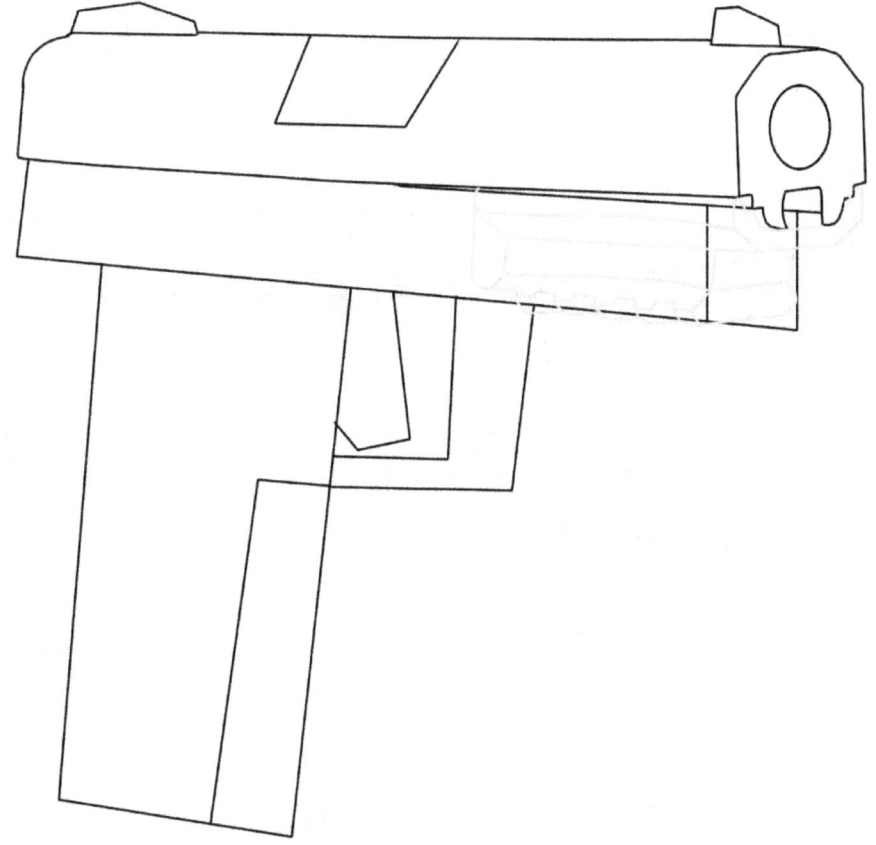

Redraw the front right below the barrel to add the support underneath it.

Step 6.

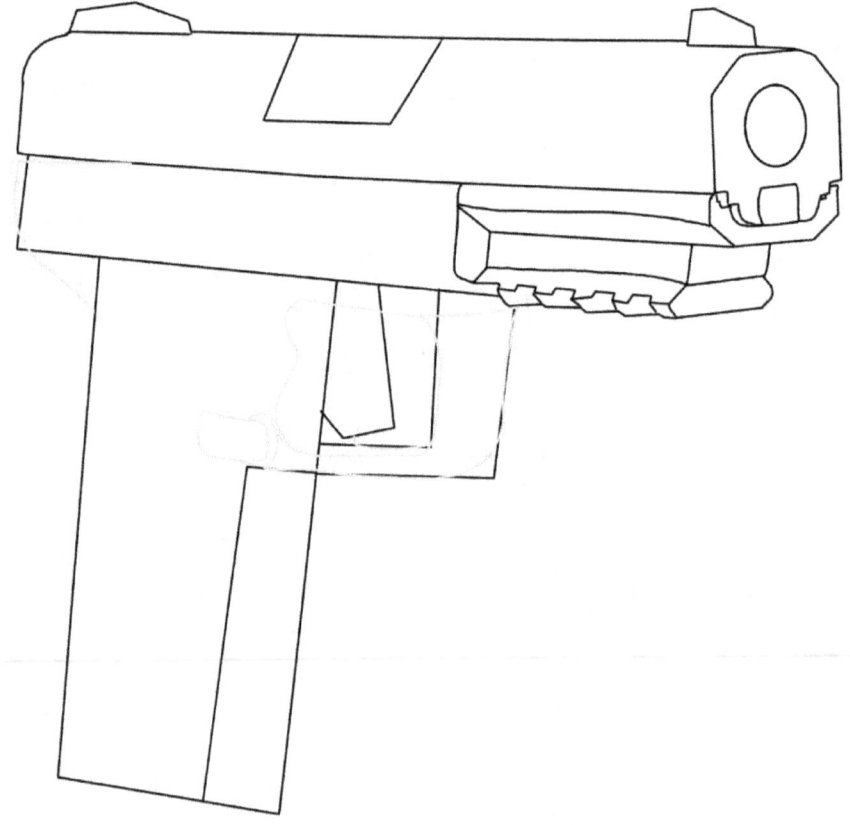

Redraw the cover of the trigger as in the example and add the
back part to the support section of the barrel.

Step 7.

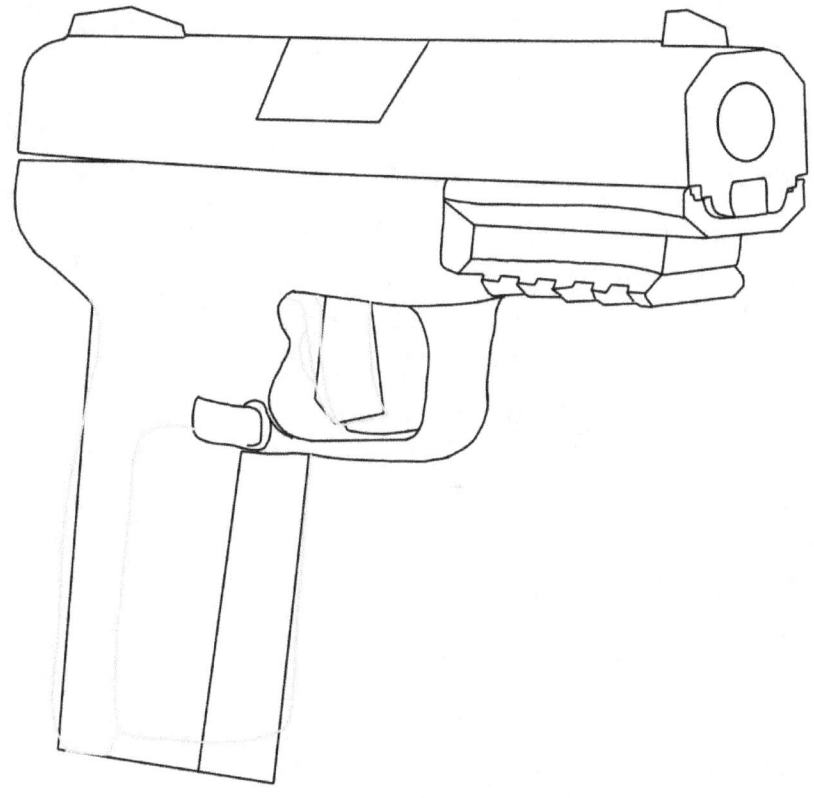

Redraw the trigger to smooth it out, and continue with redrawing the barrel as in the example.

Step 8.

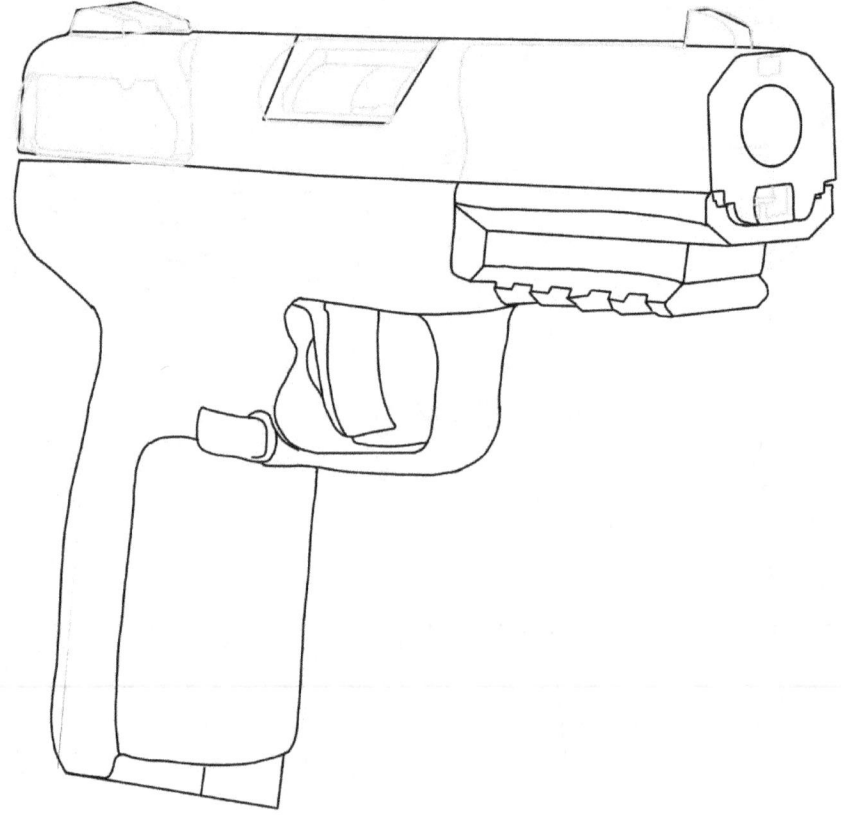

Redraw the visor and the front of the pistol to finish it.

Then add the back of the barrel where you pull the shaft back
as you load the gun.

Redraw the bullet shaft to finish it. Looking good, isn't it?

Step 9.

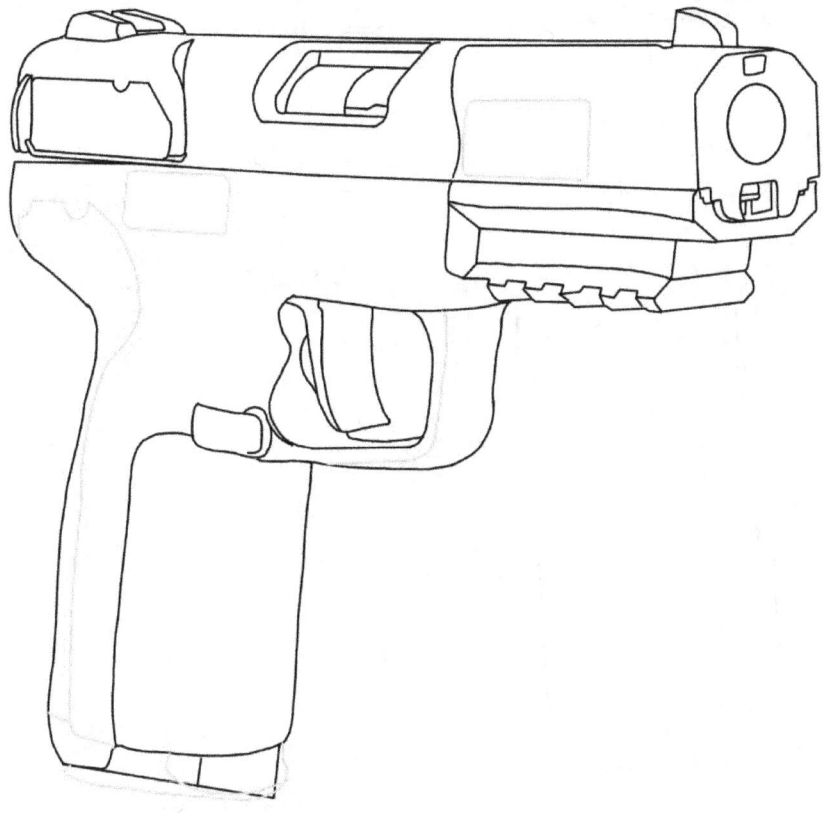

Add the detail to the front and the back.

Then add the detail to the handle.

Step 10.

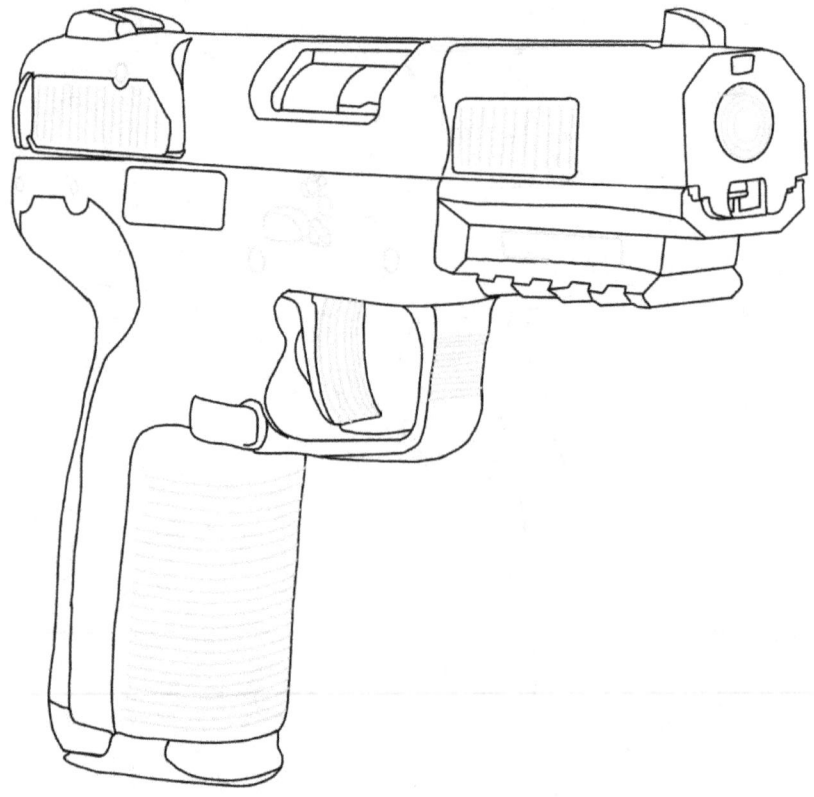

Finish the gun by adding the safety mechanism on the side.

Then add the lines which will help the hand retain grip as it

operates the weapon.

Add the inside of the barrel as in the example.

Step 11.

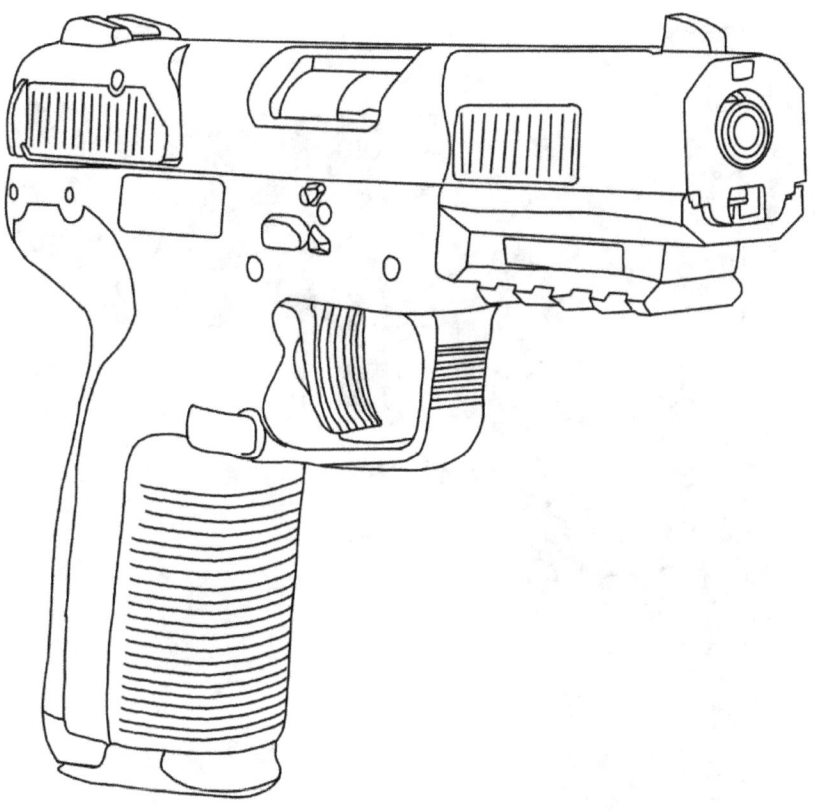

All done! Let's color!

Step 12.

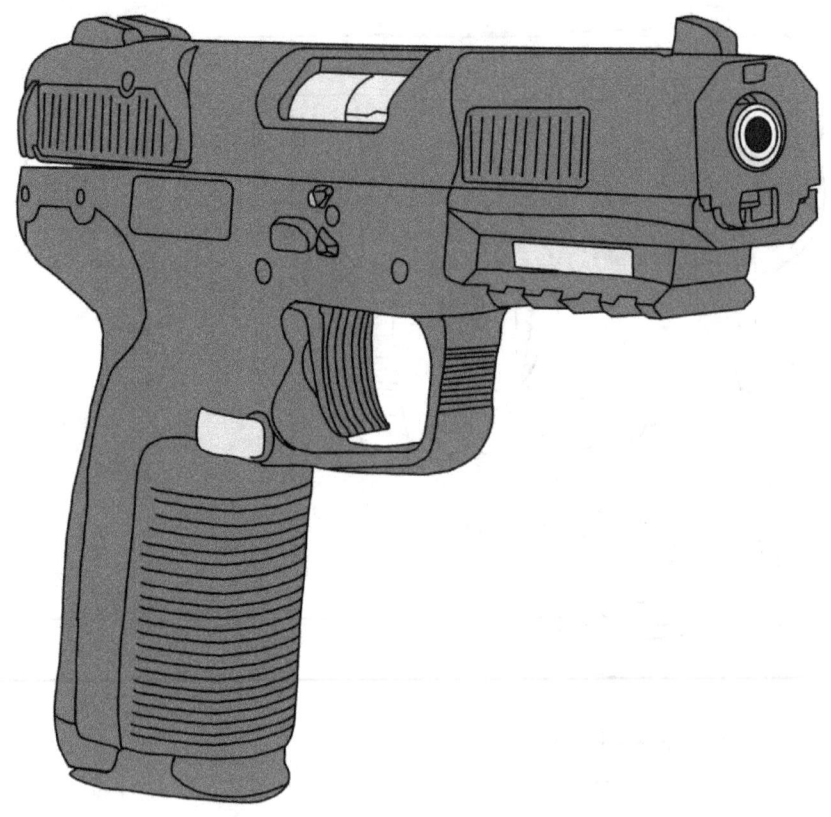

The pistol is a mono-color. Color it dark grey, with silver for the metal parts.

Step 13.

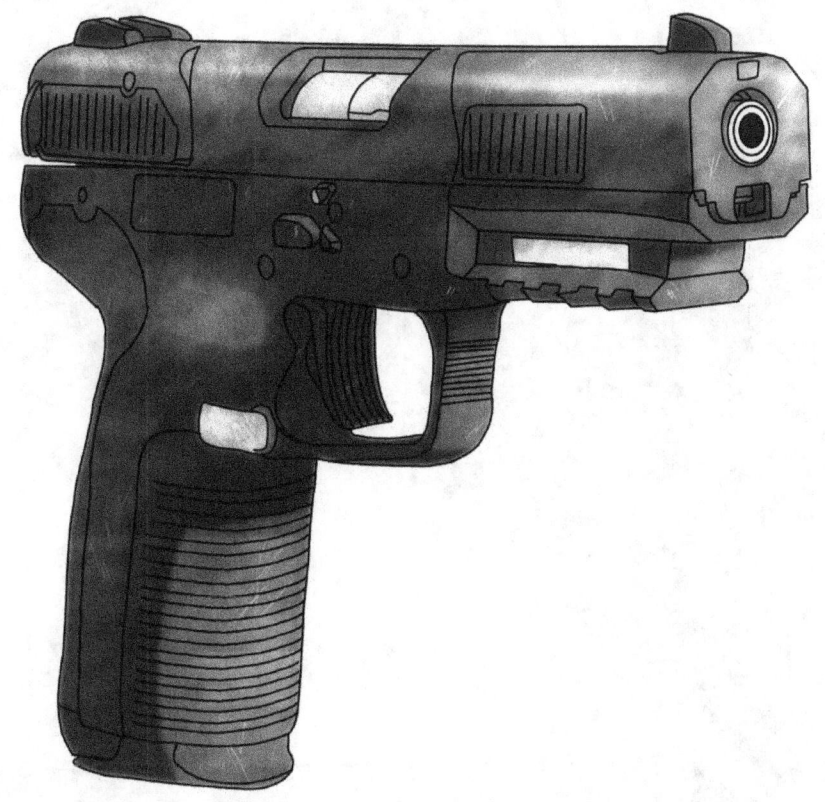

Add some color and scratches for detail. How does yours look?

Step 14.

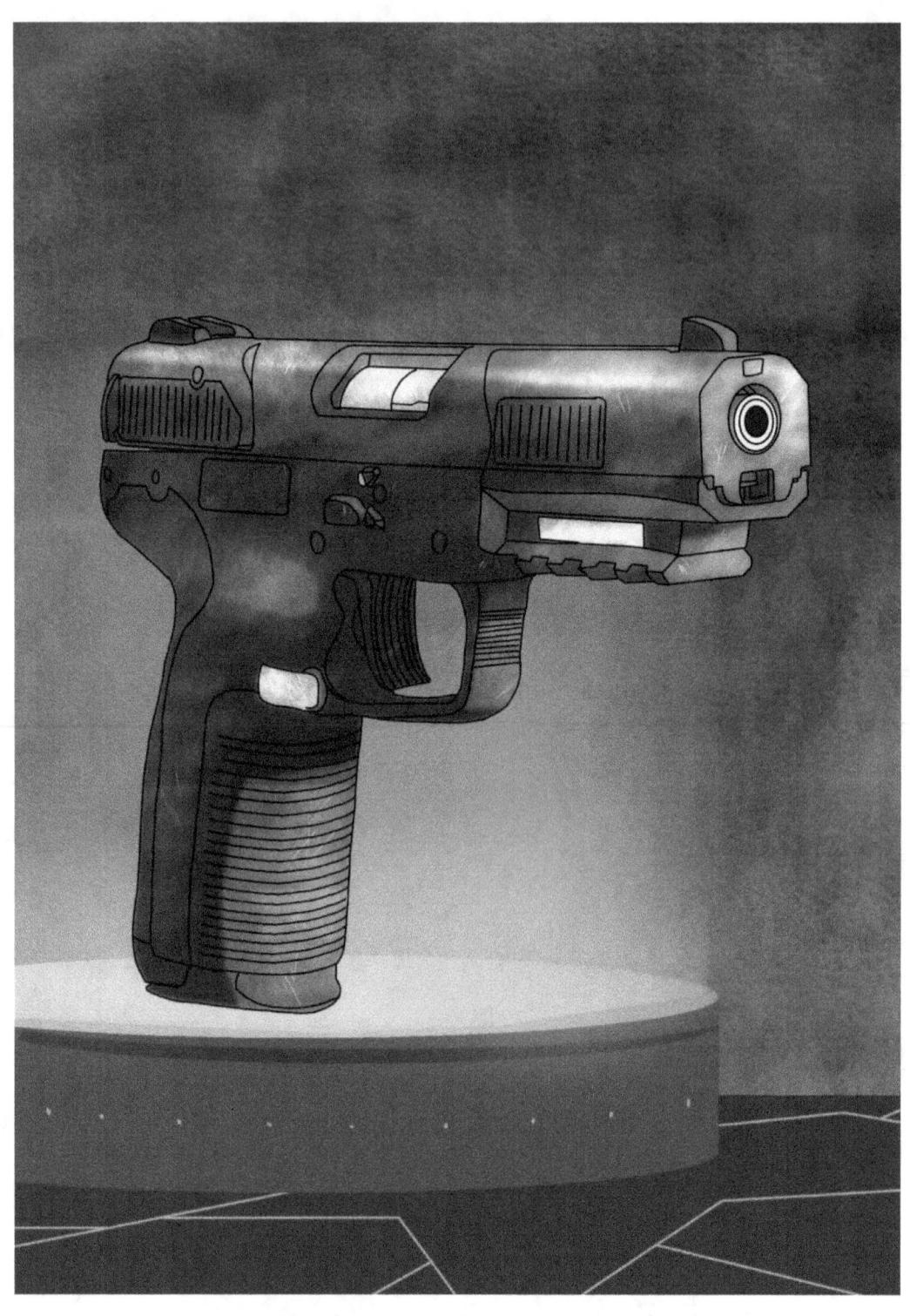

Colored version.

Step 15.

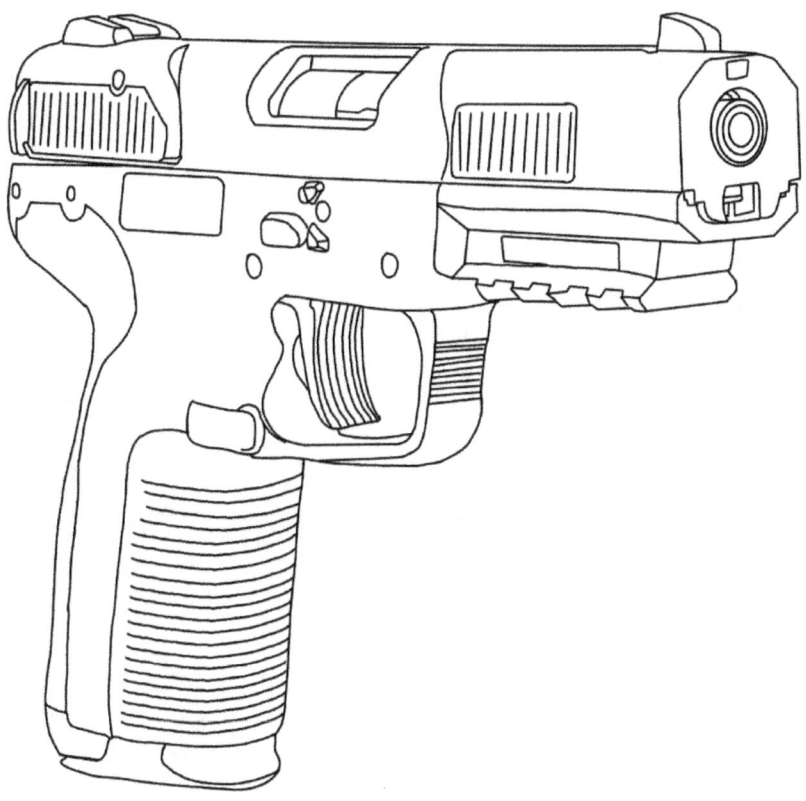

Line art version.

How to Draw a FN P90 Rifle

Step 1.

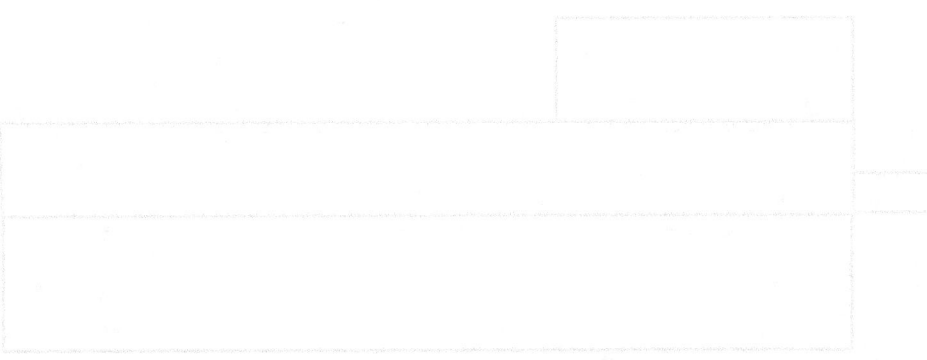

To start we will make the outline for the barrels and the visor.

Step 2.

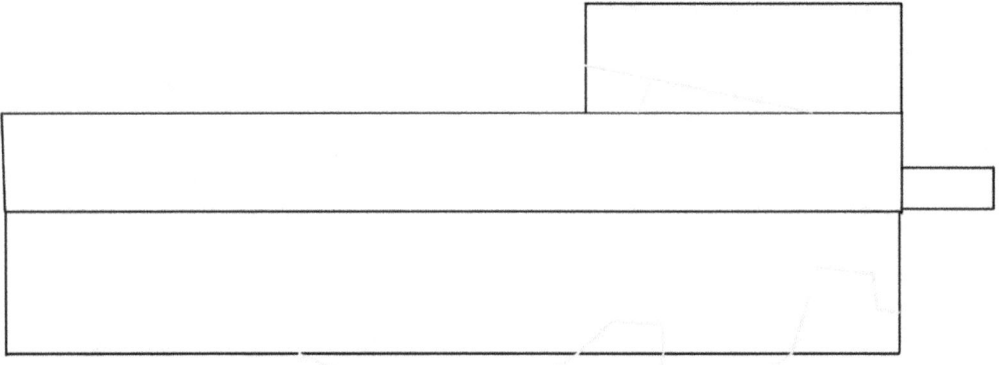

Add the slanted part to the visor and redraw the front bottom
part of the body.

Step 3.

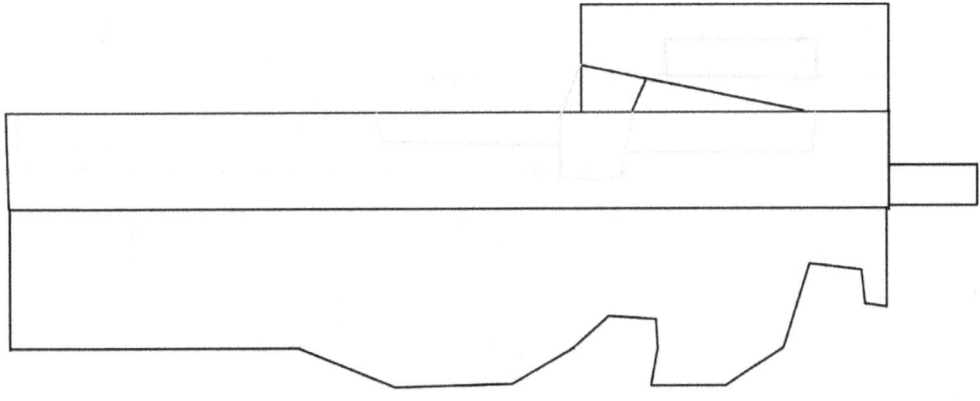

Add a rectangle to the visor and the support section to the

body.

Step 4.

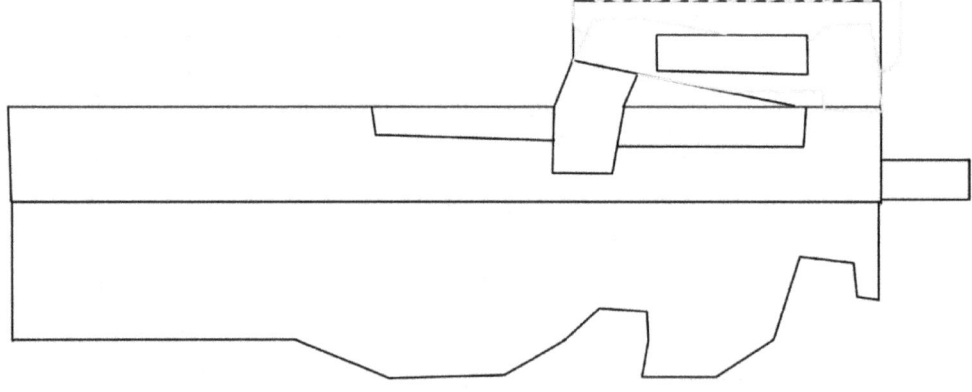

Redraw the visor. See how it has the shapes similar to the top of
a castle wall?

Step 5.

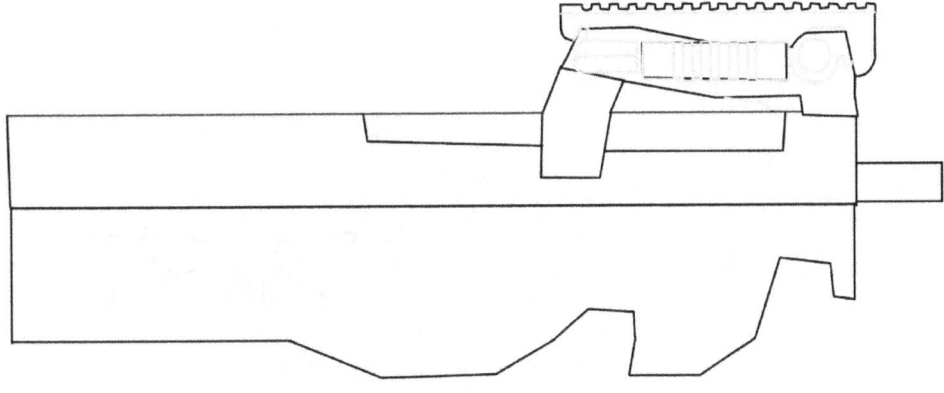

Now add the details to the visor.

Add a rectangle to the back of the visor, this will be an opening.

Step 6.

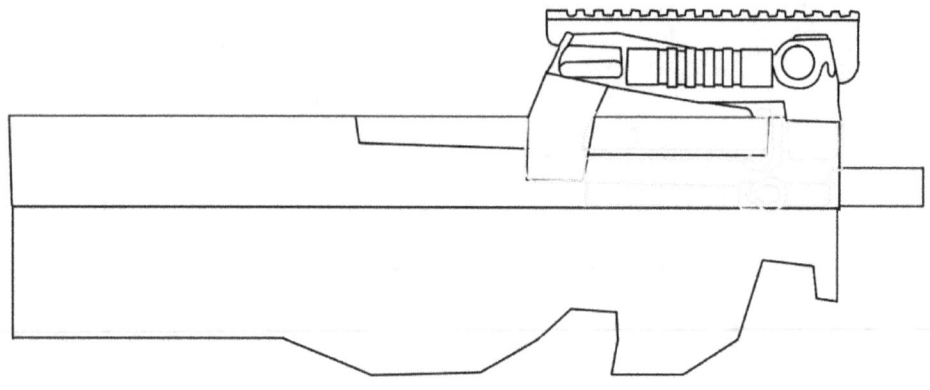

Now redraw the part of the body that holds the magazine. Make sure to use the example to help you along.

Step 7.

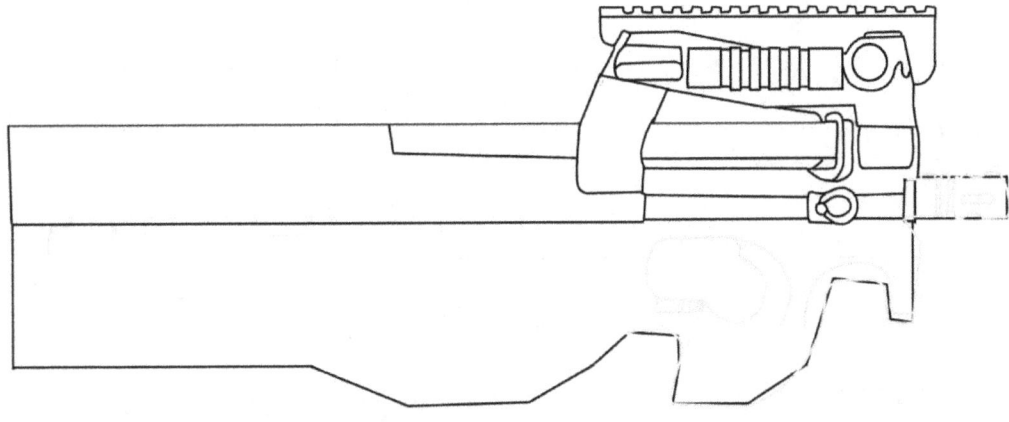

Redraw the front of the barrel. Then add the misshaped hole in the middle to where the hand holds the gun. Then reshape the bottom front part.

Step 8.

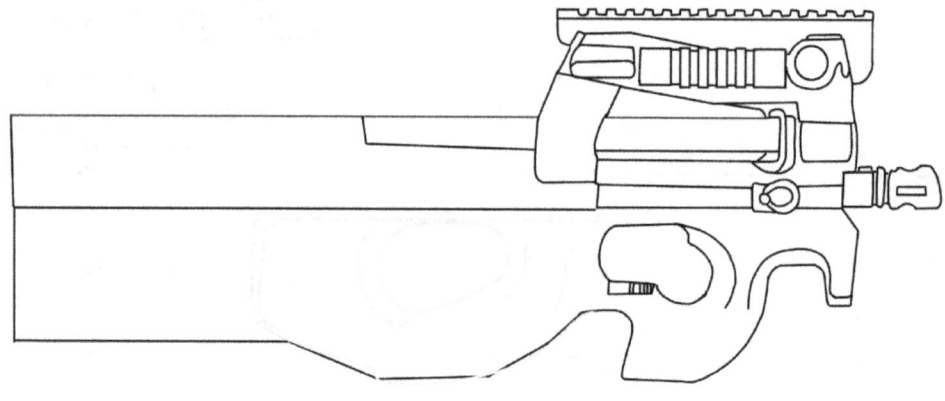

Now redraw the midsection to where the other hand goes.

Make sure to smooth out the bottom.

Step 9.

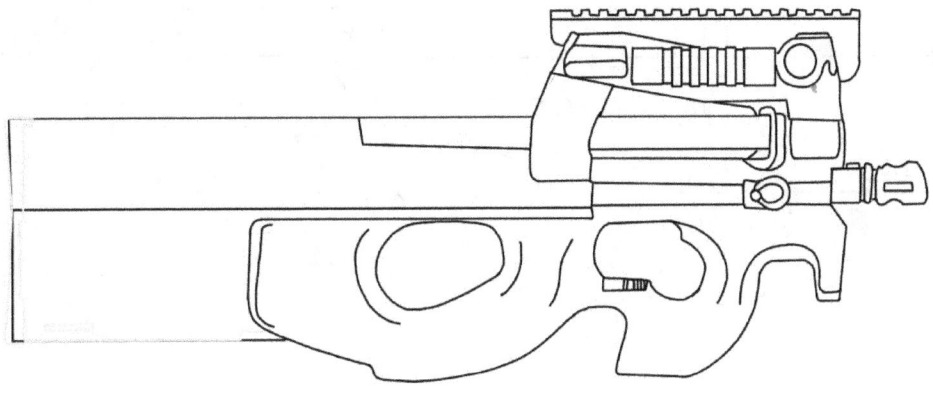

Now it's time to redraw the back of the gun as shown in the
example.

Step 10.

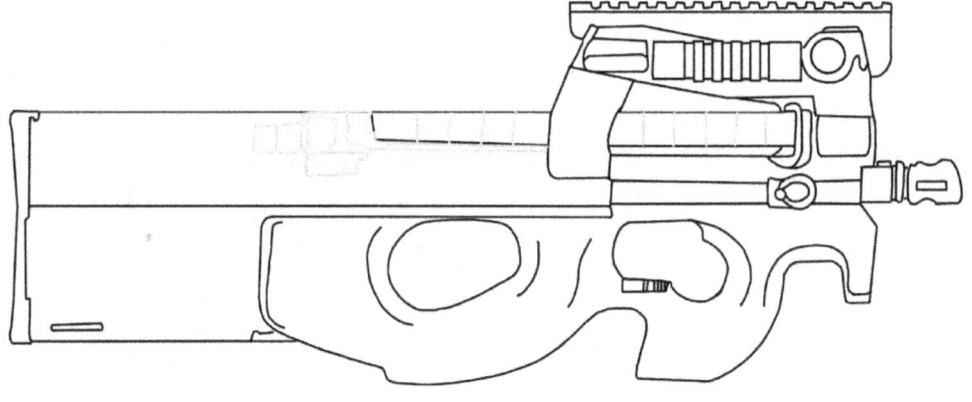

Now redraw the part which holds the magazine. See how it has

lines down the middle?

Step 11.

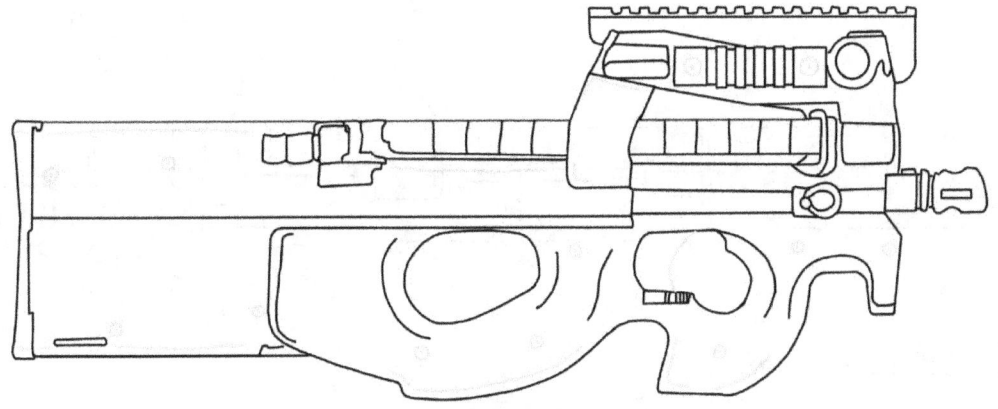

Now add the details such as the bolts to hold the gun together.

Add the lines to show that the body is curved.

Step 12.

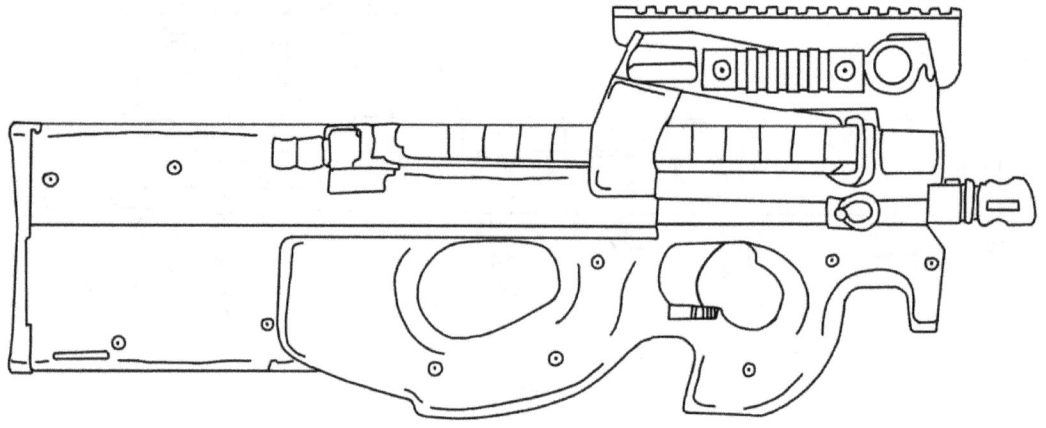

All done! Let's color!

Step 13.

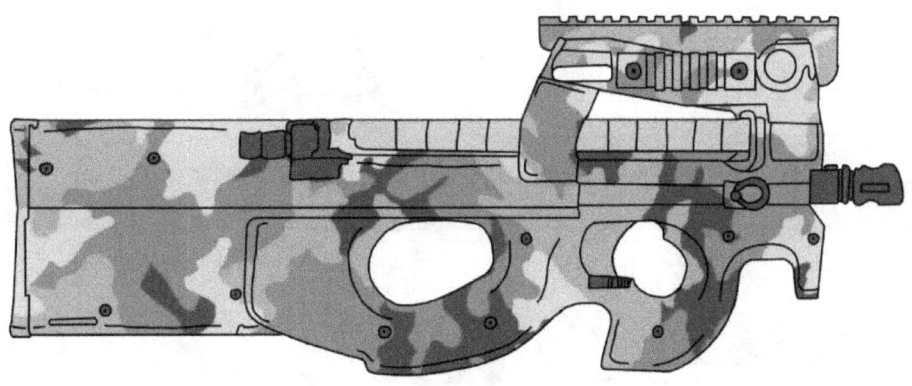

We'll make this gun a lot more colorful than the other two.

Using different shades of pink, color in blobs of what looks like blurred out leafs.

Make the magazine a light grey and the metal parts dark pink.

Step 14.

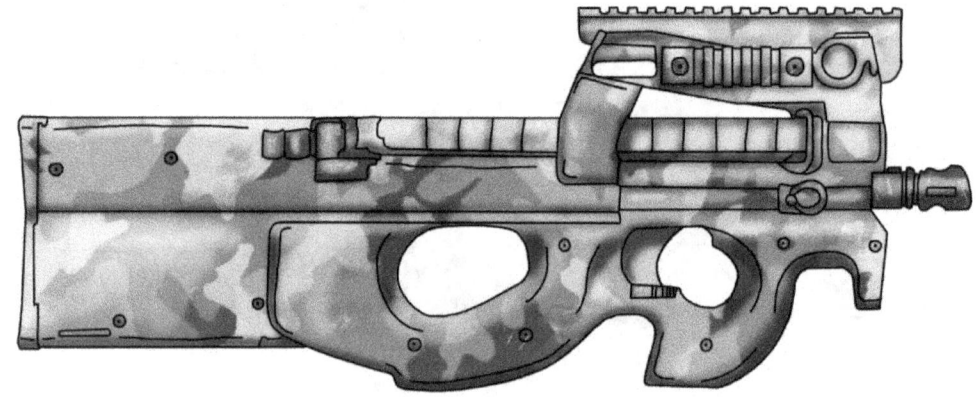

Add some color and scratches for detail. How does yours look?

Step 15.

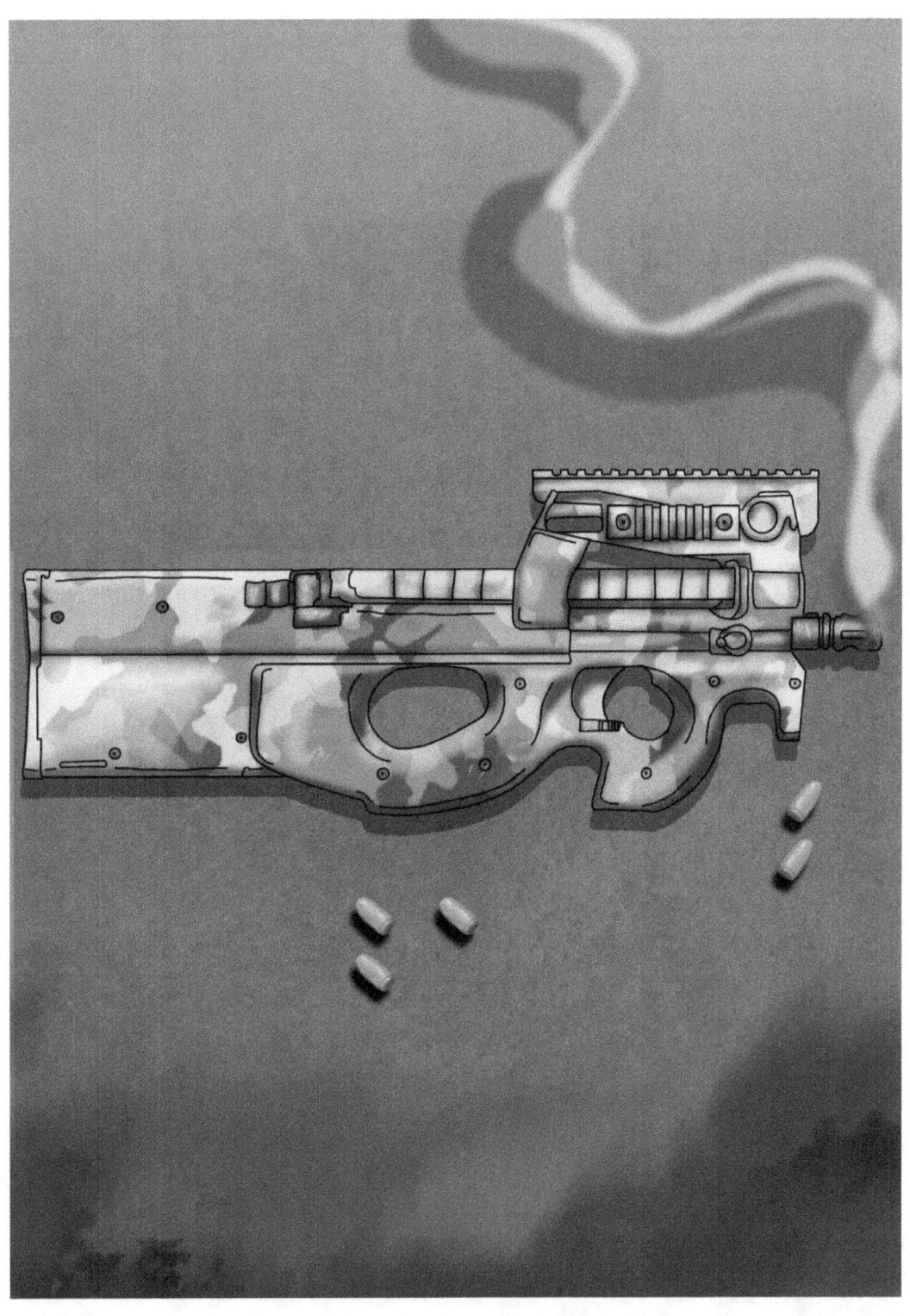

Colored version.

Step 16.

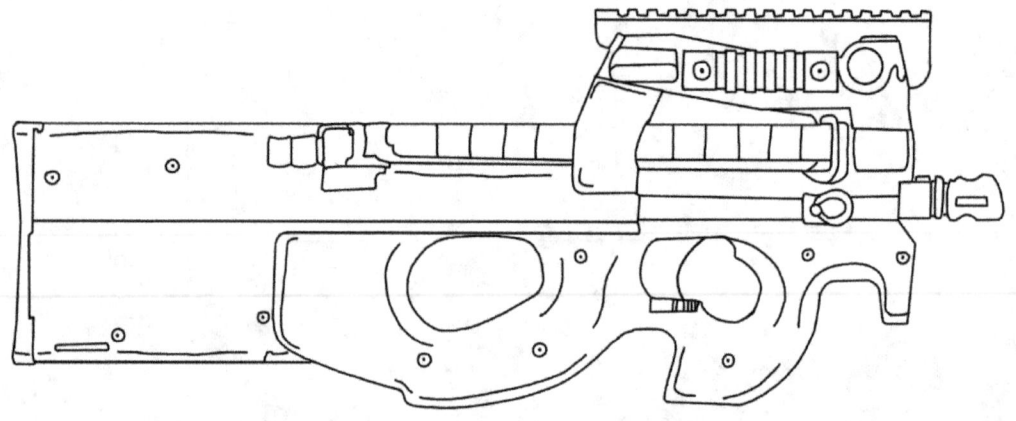

Line art version.

About the Author

Andy Hopper is an American illustrator born in sunny California just a hair's breadth from the beautiful Sierra foothills. After studying Design and Media at UCLA, Andy decided to try his hand at teaching his own unique style of art to novice artists just starting out with their craft.

He has won numerous art awards and has several publications in print and e-book to his credit. His e-books teach the beginner artist how to draw using simple techniques suitable for all ages. While Andy prefers using chalk, pencil and pastels for his own artwork, but has been known to dabble in the world of watercolour from time to time and teach this skill to his students.

Andy Hopper lives just outside of Los Angeles in Santa Monica, California with his wife of 15 years and their three children. His art studio is a welcome respite to the area and he has been known to start impromptu outdoor art sessions with the people in his neighborhood for no charge.

www.ingramcontent.com/pod-product-compliance
Lightning Source LLC
Chambersburg PA
CBHW080840170526
45158CB00009B/2596